Heavy and Light

by Rod Theodorou and Carole Telford

Contents

First published in Great Britain by Heinemann Library
an imprint of Heinemann Publishers (Oxford) Ltd
Halley Court, Jordan Hill, Oxford OX2 8EJ

MADRID ATHENS PARIS FLORENCE PRAGUE WARSAW
PORTSMOUTH NH CHICAGO SAO PAULO SINGAPORE TOKYO
MELBOURNE AUCKLAND IBADAN GABORONE JOHANNESBURG

Illustrations by Gwen Tourret and Trevor Dunton
Colour reproduction by Track QSP
Printed in China

99 98 97 96
10 9 8 7 6 5 4 3 2 1

ISBN 0 431 06394 X

British Library Cataloguing in Publication Data
Telford, Carole
 Heavy and Light. – (Animal Opposites Series)
 I. Title II. Theodorou, Rod III. Series
 591

Photographic acknowledgements
Andrew Plumptre/OSF p4; Stan Osolinski/OSF p5; Carol Farneti/Partridge Films Ltd/OSF p6;
Michael Fogden/OSF p7; Bruce Davidson p8, back cover; Robert A Tyrrell/OSF pp9, 13, 15, 17, 21;
Root/Okapia/OSF p10; Marie Read/Bruce Coleman Ltd p11; Richard Packwood/OSF pp12, 14, 20; Daniel J
Cox/OSF p16; Tom Leach/OSF p18; Jen and Des Bartlett/Bruce Coleman Ltd p19
Front cover: Mark Petersen/Tony Stone Images; Robert A Tyrell/OSF

rhino

hippo

elephant seal

Some animals
are heavy.
Some animals are light.

butterfly

bat

hummingbird

3

This is a hippopotamus.
Hippos are big and heavy.

This is a hummingbird.
Hummingbirds are
small and light.

Hippos live in Africa.
They like to live by a river.

Most hummingbirds live in
hot countries.
Many live in North and
South America.

Big hippos are very heavy.
They weigh as much as 50 people!
Even lions do not attack them.

Hummingbirds are the
smallest birds.
Some are as light as butterflies.

Hippos move slowly on land.
Under water they can move fast.

Hummingbirds fly very fast.
Their wings flap so quickly they
make a humming sound.

Hippos have special big teeth to scare off enemies.
They have other strong teeth to chew plants.

Hummingbirds
have long bills
and very long
tongues.
This helps them
to reach inside
flowers to feed.

bill

tongue

13

Hippos spend most of the
day in the water.
The water keeps them cool.

Hummingbirds are always on
the move.
They spend most of the day feeding.

Hippos need to eat lots of plants. They come out of the water every night to feed.

Hummingbirds
eat insects and
spiders.
They suck
sweet
nectar
from inside
flowers.

Hippos have one baby each year.
Even baby hippos love the mud!

Hummingbird nests are smaller than an egg cup. They lay one or two tiny eggs each year.

Sometimes baby hippos climb on adult hippos to keep safe from crocodiles.

5-day-old chicks

The mother
hummingbird
looks after
her tiny
chicks.
She brings
them insects
to eat.

AMAZING FACTS!

Hippo tusks are as long as your arm!

Hippos can hold their breath for 5 minutes.

Hummingbirds are the only birds
that can fly backwards!

Some hummingbirds steal flies
from spiders' webs!

Index